Stop Beating That Lady

—ɯ—

R J Jordan

Stop Beating That Lady

Copyright © 2014 R J Jordan

All rights reserved.

Published by Sturtevant & MacCulloch, Inc., P.O. Box 9723, Wyoming, MI 49509

This publication contains the opinions and ideas of its author. The activities outlined in this book may not be suitable for every individual, and are not guaranteed or warranted to produce any particular results. The names and identifying characteristics of individuals and locations referenced in this publication have been changed.
Permission to reproduce or transmit this publication in any form or by any means, electronic or mechanical, including photocopying and recording, or by any information storage and retrieval system, must be obtained in writing from the author, R. J. Jordan.
The author and publisher make no representations or warranties with respect to the accuracy or completeness of the contents of this book and specifically disclaim any implied warranties of merchantability or fitness for a particular purpose. Neither the publisher nor the author shall be liable for any loss of profit or any other commercial damages, including but not limited to special, incidental, consequential, or other damages.

Cover photograph by Birdalone Photography
On the cover, author, R. J. Jordan

The author may be contacted at:
r.jrdn2741@gmail.com

Additional copies of this title may be purchased at Amazon.com

ISBN-13: 978-0-692-31833-1
ISBN-10:   0-692-31833-X

ALSO BY R J JORDAN

<u>Running with the Big Dog:</u>
<u>True Stories from the Road with America's Bus Company</u>

Special thanks to:

LIVE.DANCE.MOVE

in Grand Rapids, MI, for
getting me in shape for the cover.

Contents

Preface   xi

PART ONE – FAMILY KNOWLEDGE   1

EVERYBODY'S DOING IT   3
NOBODY ASKED   7
SHUT UP   11
GUILTY PLEASURE   14
WATCH OUT   17
Family Photo   22

PART TWO – JUST K.I.S.S.
(Keep It Simple....)   23

WHAT THE HECK   25
DID YOU SEE THAT   28
GOTTA HAVE IT   30
I DON'T COUNT   32

PART THREE – MOVE ON 35

HIS FIXATION 37
DON'T HURT HER 43
WHY 46
RUN AWAY 49
HER CHOICE 52
WEIGHT FOR ME 55
DO WHAT - WHERE 58
WATCHED 60
YOU MAKE ME SICK 64
WHY NOT YOU 66
NOT ALLOWED 68

Stop Beating That Lady

PREFACE

Everyday, I overhear women commenting on what they think is wrong with their body's physical appearance. The comment can be as simple as, "a bad hair day" or as extreme as, "my body sucks." The comments come from women in all walks of life. Women that are obsessed with exercise have just as many complaints as the women that never exercise. Don't misunderstand me, there's nothing wrong with self-improvement. The problem is beating yourself up when, you think, everything is not perfect. None of us are perfect.

Most women fall somewhere in the middle of the extremes. In all fairness, women will compliment each other but, usually, in a self-deprecating way. It happens so often most don't realize they're doing it. Have you ever heard something like this? "Wow, your legs look great! I wish I could do something with my tree stumps." Of course you have, it happens everyday and no one thinks twice about it. Why do you have to take a hit when you compliment someone else?

That is what I meant by the title, "Stop Beating That Lady." It's not an outsider beating you down. It's you! Most people want to improve something about themselves, that's normal. But we have to keep things in perspective. Somehow our society has created an atmosphere where it is acceptable for women to beat themselves up.

I have watched this recurring process all of my life. Growing up with my mom, grandma, two sisters and their friends, my grandfather and I got a firsthand view of this behavior. It should not be the norm to have a self-putdown ready to counter a compliment. With the growth of social media, women are beating themselves up more than ever, in the privacy of their home. It's alright if you give or accept a compliment without adding something negative about yourself.

I am not a doctor. Nor, do I claim to be an expert in the fields discussed in this book. These are my opinions based on things I have observed and lessons I've learned through trial and error. Obstacles will come and go. Don't be an obstacle in your own life. My hope is this information will encourage you to accomplish your goals.

PART ONE

FAMILY KNOWLEDGE

EVERYBODY'S DOING IT

My grandfather was a skilled carpenter. He worked outside most of his life. I believe that is where he developed his fortitude. I was always impressed at with his skill using a hammer. He could hammer a 16-penny nail through a 2 X 4 with three hits. The amazing part was that he would not leave a mark on the wood.

When he would come home from work, in the summer, his shirt would be pretty sweaty. He usually wore those navy blue work shirts. I noticed his shirts always had white rings around the sweaty spots, when the sweat dried. The rings were always there and, as a kid, I didn't think anything of it. I think the adults assumed it was just salt left over from the sweat and it was normal.

In my neighborhood, diabetes was called "sugar." No one ever said diabetes. "Sugar" was a pretty common aliment in our neighborhood. It was just a fact of life. It didn't seem to be a big concern for anyone. Then one day, granddaddy came home early because he wasn't feeling well. You must understand, for my grandfather to actually say he didn't feel good, meant it was serious. He never admitted that he felt bad. He just dealt with aches and pains, colds and flu in his own way. For example, years later, I found him sitting in the snow in the backyard, breathing hard. He couldn't catch his breath. We got him to the hospital and found out he was having a mild heart attack. It turns out, it was his third one that week! He hadn't said a word to anyone. He just dealt with it in his own way. Good thing, I happened to see him.

When they went to see his doctor, his doctor was shocked. Granddaddy's "sugar" count was so high the doctor couldn't believe he was standing, not to mention, he drove to the doctor. Grandma never drove. She didn't even have a license. The doctor told them my grandfather should be admitted to the hospital, immediately. They had to bring his count down or my grandfather would be dead in a week.

After some discussion with my grandmother, the doctor agreed to let him go home under one condition. They had to follow a strict diet to the letter. The big focus of the diet was the elimination of all salt and sugar. He could not have any type of junk food or drinks, either. A few days later, his count had dropped significantly. Soon he was back to his old self. But he did have to take a pill for the rest of his life.

That was when I first realized that what we ate could affect how our bodies performed. I began to wonder, what would happen if all of the people around me with "sugar" started eating like granddaddy? As a kid, it was just one more thing to question in the world. I was one of those kids that asked why things were the way they were. A few days later, I was thinking about something else. None of the adults seemed to even consider it.

Looking back on it, I think at that time "sugar" was just accepted as normal because so many people had it. (There are a lot more diabetics, now). The diet the doctor had given my grandfather was thought of as his "treatment" for his ailment. But it was so much more! It wasn't a "diet." It was a LIFESTYLE CHANGE. My grandfather never went back to his old eating habits. Even though my grandmother made sure my grandfather stuck to his diet, the rest of us continued to eat the old way with sugar and salt added.

Eating healthy should not be considered a "diet." It's a lifestyle change. A "diet" implies once you reach your goal you can return to your old habits. WRONG! If you return to your old habits, your old problems will come back, too. You don't have to cut out everything you like because that won't last, either. A good lifestyle change in the way you eat is not an all or nothing proposition. Extreme changes will not be maintained for that very reason. They're too extreme and soon you will become frustrated and quit. The best way to begin is to just start eating healthier. You already have an idea of what foods are healthy. And drink more water. Ask yourself do you really want a snack? Or are you eating it because it's there. Usually it's the latter. If your resistance is low, don't buy it. If it's not in the house, it's easier to resist the urge. Start small and before you know it you'll be making the change. Keep things simple. It will be a lot easier to maintain and it will not become a chore.

Once my grandfather started eating healthy on a regular basis, he could eat some junk food without risking his life. I also find it interesting that as high as his count was, he only had to take a pill. He never had to give himself insulin shots. Insulin shots seem to be the common treatment, today. It's the balance of not going overboard on healthy food or junk food that will make a lifestyle change work.

NOBODY ASKED

Aunt Cecilia, my grandmother's sister, always had problems with her legs. Her legs were always covered with bandages between her knees and ankles. She could get around, just slowly. She lived in Maryland with her husband. We usually visited them in the summer, every year, for about 10 years. Never once during that time did we ever see her without the bandages.

They didn't have much money but they always made sure our visits were a lot of fun. Because they didn't have much money, Aunt Ceil would go to a free clinic at a renowned hospital for check ups on her legs. No one ever questioned her treatment because the hospital had a stellar reputation. She went to the clinic every month or so for at least 15 years. Aunt Ceil had a different doctor, every visit. I'm sure the doctors were on some type of rotation. She said the doctors were always very nice and caring. We all assumed that the doctors checked her for anything that might be the cause of the ulcers on her legs. No one ever asked any real questions, including my aunt and her husband.

This particular day when she went clinic, things were different. The new doctor read her records and removed the bandages from her legs. Her legs had open wounds in various stages of healing, as usual. This doctor noticed something missing from her records. So he asked her if she had ever been tested for diabetes. She said, "Sugar? Oh no. I don't have "sugar." He asked her again if she had been tested for it. Aunt Ceil admitted she didn't know. He tested her for diabetes.

The test results came back a few days later. Diabetes or "Sugar", whatever you call it, she had it. The whole family was surprised! My aunt had seen countless doctors over the years and only one thought to test her for diabetes. I remember being shocked when I heard. But I wasn't shocked that she was a diabetic. I was amazed that she hadn't been tested all of those years. I couldn't understand how that was possible. It still amazes me. How could a new doctor examining a new patient not check all of the obvious stuff first? The fact that Black Americans have a higher rate of diabetes than other Americans is one more reason she should have been tested for it. With so many diabetic friends and family, I was also surprised no one in the family thought about it, either. It was just an accepted fact of life.

The doctor told her she needed to change what she ate and cut out salt and sugar. He explained that her diabetes was affecting her body's ability to heal itself. It also was the cause of the fluid build up in her legs. He assured her that if she changed her eating habits her legs would heal up.

Stop Beating That Lady

Aunt Ceil followed the doctor's advice and changed her eating habits. It was hard at first because, back in the day, there were not a lot of healthy options in the grocery stores. She stopped frying food and stopped using salt and sugar. Not using salt was the hardest thing for her. She also reduced her pop/soda and drank more water. After approximately two months, she began to see her wounds heal up and not return. After a year, her legs were completely healed. The swelling in her feet and legs had also gone away. Her legs and feet had been swollen for so long that she forgotten they were swollen. And when the swelling went down, she cried because she couldn't believe the difference. The swelling had, literally, doubled the size of her legs and feet.

Of course, hindsight is 20-20. Just because something is out in the open doesn't mean it has been addressed. Diabetes had become so commonplace, no one thought about it. I'm not taking shots at the doctors in the clinic. I am pointing out how we should question things we don't understand. Sometimes the volume of patients can be overwhelming for the doctors and nurses. They are human, too. A few questions from a patient or family member could be just the catalyst needed to see things differently.

Too often, women feel if they ask a lot of questions they'll be dismissed as a complainer or a bitch. Society is improving, but that belief is still out there. Women are still hesitant about questioning their doctors regarding their own health. They'll ask about their family members but not about themselves. Ask! You matter!!! Don't be afraid to ask questions about your health. Most doctors have no problem explaining things to their patients. In fact, they want you to understand what's going on in your body. Doctors can't address your concerns or answer your questions, if you don't ask. Questions you have about you ARE important. Ask.

SHUT UP

Grandma's doctor's office was in the Fisher Building. The Fisher Building is an architectural gem, in Detroit. I always got the feeling that my grandmother thought he was a better doctor because his office was in the Fisher Building. She always said he was a very good doctor.

My grandmother always had a touch of arthritis and was overweight. Suddenly, her health began to change. It was becoming increasingly more difficult for her to get around. Her knees seemed to ache all of the time. It didn't matter if she was walking or sitting, they hurt. Then, her wrists began to stiffen up at random times. What had changed? What was the cause of this new pain?

She asked her doctor what was going on. He told her she was too heavy and needed to lose weight. He didn't examine her at all. A few months went by and her pain had gotten worse. She went back to her doctor. Again without examining her, he told her she needed to lose weight. She asked why he didn't examine her. He told her that he had been seeing her for years and didn't need to examine her. As crazy as that may sound, she accepted that answer. After she told us what the doctor said, she added he was the doctor and knew what he was talking about. I could tell she wasn't happy with that answer but she accepted it.

Now, Grandma could barely walk and was using a cane. She told her doctor something else had to be going on in her body. He told her, "Hilda, you are just too fat and you need to shut your mouth. You eat too much." Holy crap! What doctor would say that to a patient? She was pissed and walked out of his office. When she got in the car, she said she was going to get a new doctor. And that's exactly what she did.

Her new doctor told her it was a combination of things causing her increasing pain. The primary cause was what she had been eating. Her LDL cholesterol (the bad kind) was high and her blood pressure was a little high. Surprisingly, she did not have diabetes. He assured her that he could help her. He instructed her to reduce her sugar intake and stop using salt altogether. He also told her that salt was in everything we purchased at the grocery store. The doctor gave her a list of healthy alternatives to what she had been eating. It was funny because she realized the doctor's recommendations were almost the same as the meals she had been preparing for my grandfather.

A month later, during her follow up visit, the doctor discovered that she had pinched a nerve in the palm of her right hand. She pinched the nerve by leaning on the cane, more and more, as the pain in her legs increased. Fortunately, grandma started to feel better and the doctor suggested she try walking without the cane. She never used a cane again. Over time, the nerve, in her hand, returned to normal.

After three months, her lifestyle change was starting to pay off. Her joint pain was almost gone. She was walking better than she had in years. She even dropped a few pounds. Six months later, she had improved 100%. She had more energy and could get around without any problems. A year later, she was 50 pounds lighter.

No matter how much respect or admiration you have for someone, they do not have the right to be disrespectful to you. In fact, sometimes people are aware of how you feel about them and think your feelings allow them to walk on you. No one is better than you. Period. No matter how you feel about a person, when they take advantage of you, they have proven they don't really care about you. They wouldn't intentionally hurt, use or disrespect you, if they truly cared. When they do, you need to make a change.

Change is not easy. Because you care about the abuser, you tend to give them the benefit of the doubt. This doubt allows their poor treatment of you to continue. Be honest with yourself. When the time for a change comes, you need to do it. You have to think of yourself and what is best for you. No one can make the change for you. There are support groups and encouragement out there. But you are the only one that can make the change. Control your fear. You can do it. If the change is good for you, it's good for the people that really care about you, too. People that truly care about you want you to be well and happy.

GUILTY PLEASURE

She had been hit for the last time. He was stunned, as he tumbled down the stairway from the second floor to the first. When he landed at the bottom, he looked up into the barrel of a loaded shotgun. My grandfather said, "Time for you to go." My father got up slowly and backed out of the front door. That was the first story my sister's and I were told that confirmed my father had hit my mother.

My grandparent's owned a two-family flat. We moved in after my father squandered all the money. My grandmother told me that she bought the two-family flat because she knew we were going to need a place to live. My father was a good manipulator. He was not a good person. For every dollar my parents earned, my father wasted more than half. There were times we didn't have enough to eat. And that's crazy when you have two working parents. Eventually, his stupidity caused us to lose the house.

Once my father was gone for good, things began to improve for my mom. As you can imagine, those first few years were rough for her. She had to make some hard choices. It was not easy to take steps to change a situation that was not good for us. My father never did pay child support. And at times, my grandmother would be pretty mean to my mom. As kids, we just went with the flow.

We may know something is not good for us. But, we know what to expect and can prepare for it. If we decide to change things, we have no idea what will happen. Too often, we allow that single thought to stop us from making a change we know will be better for us. Don't allow the fear of the unknown to stop you. Trust your gut feelings. If you know you should make the change, make the change. It may be hard at first but in the long run it will be worth it.

As things continued to improve, food had become an escape for my mom. Years later she told me, "Once we got where we could eat without worrying, we were going to eat whatever we wanted." I totally understood what she meant. She had struggled and worked hard for us to have a normal life. The fact that we couldn't always eat well, when my father was acting a fool, had a significant impact on her. Being able to eat whatever she wanted was her reward for surviving an extremely difficult period in her life.

A lot of people going through rough patches in their lives turn to food for solace. When life is extremely rough, it can feel like we don't have control over anything. We just respond to the crap that's happening to us. But when we eat, we're in control. It may sound a little silly. But when everything feels like it's beyond our control, having control of anything becomes important.

And that gives a new meaning to eating. In addition, when we eat what we like, it gives us pleasure. Part of the pleasure is the total control we have over the what, when, where, and how much we eat. We also feel relief because the eating is not happening to us. We are choosing to do it.

But we have to be careful. After we've made it through the difficult period, the solace we found in the food can become detrimental. It can be very tempting to turn to food anytime things don't go our way. It's all right to "pig out" sometimes when we're frustrated with the ups and downs of life. But, we must control ourselves. Eating can be comforting but it doesn't resolve the problem. Take a step back. Review your actions and consider your other options. Then choose what you think will best resolve the problem.

Just because something is hard doesn't mean you can't do it. Most of the time, the difficult choice is the right choice. Choose to be in control. You do not need permission to decide what's best for you. What if you do make a bad choice? SO WHAT! The beauty of being in control is you can make another choice. Don't forget that. You can change your mind. It's up to you. Learn from your "oops" moments and keep making choices. Choose to keep control of your life. Don't worry too much about making a bad decision. Remember, not making a choice IS a choice. When it's up to you, you can always correct your decision.

WATCH OUT

Jane and my mother had been close friends for as long as I could remember. I remember them having lots of good times together. They also helped each other deal with several personal struggles. My mother and Jane decided they would try the latest weight loss program, at the time. The weight loss program was held in a nearby recreation center. They were both excited to try the new program. They joked about how good they were going to look, in the spring.

Once a week, the participants met at the rec center with the certified leader. They would swap stories of their efforts to lose weight. The leader provided guidance on proper eating and exercise. She also addressed concerns and answered questions. The participants encouraged each other to stick with the program. Jane and my mom were always energized when they returned from the meetings. It was nice to see the excitement in my mom.

They didn't lose any weight the first couple of weeks. But they stuck with it because they really did feel better. About the third week, Jane lost about three pounds. My mom lost about a pound. It didn't seem to matter. They were happy for each other. And, the whole group had started to lose weight. Their weight loss was always between one and four pounds. Jane always lost more weight than my mom. But that never bothered my mom. She was just glad the program was working. She continued to be Jane's number one cheerleader. Jane seemed happy with the results, as well.

At one weigh-in, they got a surprise. My mom lost one pound more than Jane. My mom and Jane were shocked because that had never happened. Jane seemed a little more than shocked. She seemed to be a little pissed off, too. You could see it in her face. She couldn't hide it. Even the group leader asked her if she was all right. During the ride home, Jane told my mother she could not believe she'd lost more weight then her. Jane said there must have been something wrong with the scale. Now, my mom was surprised. My mom told Jane it wasn't impossible for her to lose one pound more than she did. And, the weight loss had always been within a pound or two of each other. Besides, they both lost weight and that was the main thing. Jane didn't say another word.

The next week, Jane was late picking up my mother. But Jane did lose more weight than my mom, that week. From that day on, Jane ran 10 to 15 minutes late. Jane began to criticize the program, more and more. The program that had been fine up to that point, now according to Jane, had a new problem every week. Jane no longer lost more weight than my mom, every week. They went back and forth losing the most weight. Their weight

Stop Beating That Lady

loss stayed within a pound or two of each other. But that seemed to really piss off Jane and she couldn't hide the anger. She stopped encouraging my mom. When mom would get in the car, Jane would say things like, "Damn girl, did you forget we had to weigh in? You're looking kind of big." My mom would just laugh it off.

All of a sudden Jane was always busy on the day they were supposed to go to the weight loss program. When my mom asked her what was going on, Jane said she had stuff to do. When she did go, she would be very late. The class was only an hour long. Jane would be 30 minutes late. At that point, mom told Jane if they couldn't go on time they shouldn't go. That was fine with Jane. She stopped going.

For the next few weeks, I took my mom to the weight loss class. She was disappointed with Jane's actions and it wasn't fun for her, anymore. When Jane realized my mom was still going and losing weight, she was outraged. When they would see each other, Jane continued her not so subtle putdowns. All of Jane's insults were weight related. My mother had to tell her off a couple of times. After Jane saw that my mother was not going to put up with her insults, Jane stopped coming around. It finally got to the point where Jane stopped talking to my mother. It wasn't long before my mom became discouraged and stopped going to the weight loss class. Jane had accomplished her goal.

Jane is the perfect example of a "So Called Friend." A "So Called Friend" is your friend because they believe they are better than you. (By the way, they're wrong.) But they believe it to be true. This type of friend can hurt you because you don't see that side of them, in the beginning. You believe your friendship is on equal footing. As the friendship grows, you share personal information and form a bond.

Then one day you get something they wanted. A guy gives you a flattering glance. You get a promotion. You look great in an outfit. You lose more weight than them. It could be anything. There's no way to know what the trigger will be. But once you get what they wanted, you'll begin to notice a change in their behavior towards you.

You can only react to how they treat you. As a friend, you should question the change in behavior because there could be something else going on. After the two of you talk about it, if the answers really don't seem to make sense; you have to consider that the person may not be a true friend. When they continue to say hurtful things or use private information you've shared to embarrass you, you have to protect yourself. That person is not your friend and you have to let them go.

It won't be easy, because you are a true friend. You want to give them a chance to prove you wrong. But that person won't be happy unless they pull you down. A person that is close to you CAN pull you down. That is why you have to watch what they actually do - not what they say. Because you truly care about them, what they think of you matters. That is their leverage over you. Their actions will show how they feel about you.

No matter how you feel about them, you cannot allow them to hurt you emotionally or physically. You can stop them by ending your association with them.

You do not have to explain yourself. They know what they have been doing to you. If you try to explain, they will disagree and try to put the blame on you. Remember, they have been close to you. They know how you feel about things. They can use that knowledge to make you feel guilty. Don't fall for it. No explanation is necessary. Just let them go.

A "So Called Friend" could be anyone, including a relative or spouse. Their hurtful behavior towards you is the give away. It doesn't matter who it is. You have to let that person go once they begin to undermine you. That person CAN make you doubt your decisions. They CAN discourage you from doing things that will benefit you. They CAN make you feel bad about yourself. Don't allow them to do it! Life is hard enough. You do not need "So Called Friends" making it harder. It's up to you, not them. Let them go. You'll be happier in the long run.

<u>Family Photo</u>

Left to Right
Front Row: Me, My Great Grandmother, My Little Sister, My Grandma's Big Sister (Aunt Anita)

Second Row: My Big Sister, My Mom, My Grandmother, My Grandfather

PART TWO

JUST K.I.S.S.
(Keep It Simple....)

WHAT THE HECK

Changing your lifestyle can be very rewarding. But in the beginning, it can be a little scary and frustrating. Every expert you hear seems to contradict the last one you heard. Things that were okay, years ago, are now bad for you and vice versa. TV shows will have a segment on healthy eating or exercise. Then, the very next segment will show you how to make a great dessert. What are you supposed to do?

You've made up your mind that you are going to do it! You're going to eat better and be more active. You go to work with excitement and determination. In the back of your mind, there is a little self-doubt, too. You tell a co-worker about your decision. And she says, "That's crazy, summer's over." Well, you decide to tell another co-worker. This one says, "Good for you, that's awesome. Good luck." Now you feel a little better. A little later, someone comes up to tell you they heard you were trying to lose weight. Then they say, "There are donuts in the break room. I'd start tomorrow." Now your doubt has grown and you're not sure it's a good idea.

You've decided to do it! You're going to change your lifestyle by eating better and being more active. You tell your super healthy friend and she is genuinely excited for you. She's going to make you a list of how many calories are in your breakfast, lunch, dinner and snacks. Before you can say thanks, she volunteers to clean out your pantry. And, starts to pull items out that she thinks you shouldn't keep. Then, she stops in mid-sentence – looks at you – and screams, "We have to go shopping! You're going to need workout gear and clothes that'll show off your new figure!" Now, you're afraid and wish you never said anything.

Today is the day! You are going to change your lifestyle for the better. You're tired of being tired. You tell your spouse you want to be a better you, starting today. Your spouse smiles and says, "Great" and leaves the room. A few seconds later, they return and ask, "Why don't you wait a few weeks before you start all of that? School starts in a couple of weeks and you know how things get around here. I'm just saying." You feel the wind leave your sails. Maybe they're right. It's not the right time. When will the time be right?

At a dinner with friends, you decide to share your decision to have a healthy lifestyle. You've been friends with this group for years. A little moral support couldn't hurt. Here's the conversation:

"Oh, good for you."

"You're not fat. You're smaller than me. Are you saying I'm fat?"

"What? No. I'm talking about me. I want to feel better."

"So what do you mean by *a healthy lifestyle*? Shoot, we diet all the time."

"I wondered why you ordered fish."

"Oh, here we go! You're going to start preaching to us about what we're doing wrong."

"Yeah, don't judge me."

"No, I'm not. I want to do this for me."

These are your friends. What just happened? How did this turn into me versus them? Maybe this change thing is a bad idea.

If you want to make a positive lifestyle change, it IS a good idea. You will run into obstacles but don't let that stop you. Some of the obstacles may point to other changes that you need to make to move forward. As you move forward, you will meet people that are supportive. You will not be alone. You will find other positive people out there. And those people will reinforce your positive outlook. Don't give up.

DID YOU SEE THAT

I started reading ingredient labels for my grandmother when she had to eliminate salt from her diet. So I looked for the word "salt" or any word that had "sodium" in it. For practical purposes, they are the same. If you are trying to cut down on salt, watch out for "sodium" in the ingredients, also. Another simple way to cut back on salt is to stop adding it to your food at the table. It sounds simple. But some people have added salt, at the table automatically, for so long, they don't even think about it. It'll make a big difference.

Do not depend on the package labeling (the front of the package) to be totally honest about the ingredients. Companies can put almost anything they want on the front of a product. When you see "Sugar Free", "Lower Fat" or "Fat Free" that usually means more salt/sodium has been added. The manufacturers have to make adjustments in the recipes to keep the food tasty. You have to decide which ingredient you want the least. Sometimes the amounts in original product are about the same as the healthy one. The real question is, "Lower" or "Reduced" compared to what?

Most people are not sure how much an "mg" or "g" is when they see the unit of measure on a food label. We know what they stand for but we don't know how much that is, physically. Don't worry about it. Keep it simple. The larger the number the more is in the product. When you compare product labels, make certain the ingredient you are checking is listed with the same unit of measure, on both labels. You should not limit your comparisons to the healthy versions of a product. Check the regular version, too. Sometimes, the only difference is the price. The healthy labeled one will cost more.

Be sure to check and compare the labels on bread, too. You will be amazed at the differences in the amounts of the ingredients. By checking ingredient labels, you can make simple changes in what you eat. There are healthier versions of most things we eat each day. And they taste good. Years ago, they did not taste very good. But the food companies have done a great job improving the taste, in the last few years. Switching to healthier versions of what you're already eating will help you keep things simple. Keeping it simple will help you stick with your decision to change your lifestyle.

GOTTA HAVE IT

Another simple way to reduce your sugar intake is to stop adding sugar to your coffee or tea. Most of us overlook our daily cups of coffee or tea. If that's too big a leap, try cutting the amount in half. It's easy and it too, will make a big difference.

If you must have pop (soda), don't buy the big two-liter bottle or the standard size cans. When you buy the large size, you justify drinking it all by telling yourself you don't want it to go to waste. Purchasing the mini cans will eliminate that excuse and help you control how much you drink. Drinking a glass of water, straight down, before you drink that pop will also ease the urge.

The same philosophy works for chips. Instead of buying the big bag, get the bag that has the smaller bags of chips in it. The switch will make it easier to eat fewer chips. And none will go to waste. They also make chips with "reduced" or "no salt." Try them. They are a tasty alternative.

These simple changes help because the craving usually goes away shortly after you start eating or drinking the item. But you keep going until it's gone and that's a natural habit. The smaller size satisfies the craving and the natural desire to consume until it's gone. But, you will have consumed less.

If there are certain items that you love to eat, don't keep them in the house. You can't eat it, if it's not there. Only purchase that item in a single serve size. And consume it when you buy it. Don't buy several of the single serve size and store them at home. If you do, you will consume them without stopping, just like the large size. Consuming the single serve size when you buy it will keep you from overdoing it. The extra cost of the single size serving will also make you question if really want it. When you do make the purchase, think of it as a treat for sticking to your plan. By the way - Drinking water is ALWAYS a good idea. When you go to the restroom, look at the color of your urine. The darker it is, the more water you need to drink. When you're drinking the proper amount of water, your urine will be almost clear.

I DON'T COUNT

Why is it when we hear or read about eating healthy everyone talks about counting calories? There are times when people are training for specific athletic events where keeping track of their calories is important. But to the average person, there is no true need to count calories. When you are trying to change your eating habits, counting calories is one of the most frustrating things you can do. Think about it. Every time you get ready to eat something, you have to check your calorie chart or calorie app for the number of calories in each item. Then you add it to the total of what you've already eaten. After that, you think about what you'll be doing later that day and how this meal fits in your total calories for the day. Following that routine over and over, day in and day out, becomes something you hate. Is there any wonder why you quit after a short period of time?

There are good and bad calories. In addition to keeping track of how many calories, you need to make adjustments for the good calories. WHAT? If they're good calories, do you still add them? They're still calories. How can they not be added in the total? Are you getting confused or frustrated just thinking about it?

You do not need to count the calories of everything you eat or drink. Keep it simple. You already know what foods are healthy and which are not. Come on. You know when your portions are too large. Not to mention, the calorie count listed on the package is based on the "serving size" listed on the package. Most of the time the "serving size" is much smaller than what the average person would eat, anyway. So why count? Did you know - A bowl of ice cream has more calories than a cup of ice cream? Of course, you knew that. It doesn't matter how many calories are in the ice cream. The bowl has more. It's ice cream! You already know it's not a healthy food choice. Did you know – One piece of salmon has fewer calories than three similar sized pieces of salmon? Yes, you did. You also know that three pieces of salmon are probably more than you should eat at one time. Even if salmon is good for you, too much is still too much. Did you know – Baked or grilled chicken is healthier for you than fried chicken? I bet you did.

These examples may be a little oversimplified. But the fact is, you know a lot about things you should and should not eat. Use that knowledge to start your lifestyle change. The food that is good for you is the same food that was good for your grandparents. Time has shown us what foods are healthy. You don't have to spend weeks researching food before you begin to make some changes. That is an easy way to pretend to be working on changing your lifestyle.

Try not to over think eating healthier. Over thinking can make even simple things seem difficult. You don't need to know every possibility before you start your lifestyle change. Thinking that you do will prevent you from doing anything different. Stop preventing that lady from making her life better. You can make the change. Just start. Start with what you know. Don't over think it. Start small but start! Each step, no matter how small, will help you to achieve your desired lifestyle change. Sometimes, you can be your biggest obstacle. Move out of your way.

PART THREE

MOVE ON

HIS FIXATION

Jim was a good family friend. He watched out for us when we were young. And, he would check in on my mom and grandma from time to time, after my grandfather passed away. He always had a wild, funny story to tell when he would visit. He seemed to have an exciting life.

Jim had always been physically fit. One day, he stopped by and he looked a lot more muscular. He told us, he had begun bodybuilding. It looked like he was pretty good at it, too. He wanted to show us something outside. We thought maybe he had a new car. Nope. When we went outside, he put his car in neutral. With his outstretched arm, he grabbed the bumper and pulled the car to him. We couldn't believe it. He was doing bicep curls with his car. He did it several times. He pulled it to him and pushed it back with one arm. Wow! We were impressed.

Another time we were at Belle Isle Park, in Detroit. Belle Isle is an island park in the Detroit River, in downtown Detroit. We were enjoying the day at the park and Jim told us he was going for a run. When we looked around, he was jogging and pushing his car at the same time. He jogged and pushed his car around the whole island, nonstop. It's about two miles around the whole island. He liked taking things to the extreme.

As he continued to increase his strength, he seemed to be getting irrational. He always seemed to be looking for a way to top his last feat of strength. He was going to run out of extreme things to do, or kill himself trying. At the time, I didn't know about steroids. But I knew something strange was going on. When he would come to visit, he was the same nice guy we'd always known. But his extreme stories were changing. Instead of crazy demonstrations of his strength, he was becoming violent.

He told us about a fight he had at the gym. Jim was lifting weights in the mirror. Like most gyms, the whole wall was a mirror. A guy walked up and stood directly in front of him and started lifting weights. Jim couldn't believe it. All of that space in the gym, and the guy stops in front of him. So he told the guy to move. The guy said they should have a little contest. Whoever lifted the most weight would get the spot. Jim agreed. They started to lift. By the second round, they were bumping into each other. We told Jim that was crazy, because they both could've been hurt, playing all of that weight. Jim just smiled and kept going with the story. The two of them kept at it until they stumbled and both dropped the weights. Jim was also a very good fighter. He grabbed the guy and punched him in the face! The guy tripped and fell backwards. Jim grabbed a dumbbell and was about to hit the guy. When the manager grabbed his arm and stopped him. The manager kicked them both out of the gym, permanently. We told him he would've killed that guy, if the manager hadn't grabbed his arm. He smiled and said he was just going to scare the guy.

Jim continued to workout, more and more. His bodybuilding lifestyle had become an obsession. He even entered a few contests and did well. There were a few times he injured himself. He hated that his injuries forced him to tone down his workouts. How would he get that extreme fix, he seemed to crave so much?

We got the answer on his next visit. Jim was at the grocery store and some guy bumped his cart. The guy didn't say anything. He just kept going down the aisle. When they passed each other in the next aisle, Jim bumped the guy's cart and said it was an accident. Then he gave the guy a sarcastic apology. The guy just looked at him and walked away. After they both checked out, Jim clipped the guy's heel with his cart! The guy was about the same size as Jim but not as fit. Jim did always seem to pick guys about his size. I think in his mind that made it fair. The guy asked Jim if he had a problem. Jim said, "You're an asshole." The guy said, "Right" and turned to walk away. As the guy walked away, Jim grabbed him by the shoulder to turn him around. The guy balled up his fist, as he was turning around. But Jim punched him in the eye before he could do anything. Jim thought it was so funny. He was laughing the whole time he was telling the story. The store called the police. The police didn't arrest either one of them. Jim and the guy blamed each other. The cops told both of them to go home and stop acting like children. Jim had been lucky, again. And, he satisfied his extreme craving.

It had been almost a year since we had seen or heard from Jim. So we were surprised, when he stopped by one evening. We were glad to see him. He had changed a lot. He was smaller. And, it looked like he hadn't been working out, at all. He also had bruises on his face and head. We asked him what happened and where had he been. He told us the police beat him and locked him up about a year ago.

Jim and his wife had ups and downs like any marriage. The difference was, Jim's wife called her family every time they disagreed on anything. It was so weird. Her brothers or her father would go to Jim's house and they would all argue. They had done that for years. Jim had never been violent with his wife, despite his obsession to fight. For some unknown reason, Jim decided he was not going to put up with her family intervening, anymore.

This time when her two brothers arrived, Jim jumped on them as soon as the walked in the house. He beat the crap out of both of them. The whole time his wife was yelling at him to stop. Finally, after her brothers were beaten down, she called the police. Shortly after her call, two officers arrived, a man and a woman. As soon as the police arrived, Jim's wife ran outside yelling that Jim was crazy. And he had just beaten up her brothers. Jim was right behind her. They left the front door open and the police could see the two bodies lying on the floor. They told Jim to freeze. The lady cop was closest to Jim. So she grabbed him by his wrist and told him he was under arrest. Jim slapped her and the force knocked her down on the porch.

The other cop grabbed Jim and threw him to the ground, from the porch. As he tried to handcuff him, Jim rolled over and elbowed the cop in the face. The two men were now in a full-scale fight on the lawn. The other cop had called for backup. She grabbed Jim around the neck with her nightstick. But that didn't stop him. Somehow, he flipped her over his back. That was when the other cops arrived. They were all yelling at Jim to stop and lay down but he kept fighting. Two cops pulled him off of the officer on the ground. Jim kicked a third cop, as they pulled him up. Jim had attacked at least four cops! Had he lost his mind? According to Jim, once they restrained him, they gave him a severe beating. We just looked at him like he was crazy. What did he think was going to happen? We told him he was lucky they didn't shoot him.

They took him to jail. He had been in jail for six months. Now, he was on probation. He was pretty remorseful. He never told us what he had been taking. But, he admitted that what he was taking to get bigger made him a little crazy. A little?? He had stopped taking whatever it was that made him so big. He was glad that he survived the ordeal.

When he first started to see results from working out, it made him feel great. He had never felt like that. So, he wanted to recreate that feeling. In his mind, he could only recreate that initial feeling by surprising people with his physical development. His initial physical change received such a great reaction, he was willing do anything to keep getting bigger. His lifestyle change went from positive personal growth to an unhealthy, extreme obsession. Even though he could see things taking a bad turn, he ignored the signs and paid the price.

DON'T HURT HER

Becoming active is essential in changing your lifestyle for the better. But you have to be careful, especially in the beginning. You could easily get caught up in the excitement of self-improvement. When you begin to see results from your hard work, it will excite you. That excitement will motivate you to continue. You may even want to do more. And that is great.

You're eating better, becoming more active and even feeling better. Now the adrenaline really gets pumping and you want better results, faster. There's no harm in pushing yourself. But be careful, your body is not use to all of that new activity you're introducing to it. Steady progression is the best way to maintain any changes you make. You may not want to hear this, but more than likely, steady progression is exactly how your life changed before you realized it. You cannot reverse all of the changes overnight. Taking extreme measures to get quicker results is a bad idea.

If you get too active too fast, you can get physically injured. Your body will let you know what it can handle. Listen to your body. When you start to feel pain, stop. Pain is your body's way of letting you know you've reached your limit. A better way to gauge your activity is by next day soreness. If you felt you were at your limit, while you were exercising, you probably were. The next day, the muscles you worked will be sore. A little soreness is a sign of growth. Pain is an alarm for an injury. You will be able to tell the difference. Your body will always respond to increased physical activity. Don't worry. Becoming more active is a good idea. Pushing yourself to the extreme is not.

The leaps in technology, our society has made over the last 10 years, have conditioned us to expect instant results. Instant results are not a realistic expectation when you are making physical changes in your body. You didn't gain the unwanted weight overnight. You didn't just stop being active overnight, either. The changes happened a little bit at a time. And before you knew it, things had completely changed. Becoming more active will help you reverse those unwanted changes to your lifestyle.

You may come across information regarding exercise that talks about pushing yourself to "complete exhaustion" or keep going until you reach "total muscle failure." Those are bad ideas, especially when you're just starting out. In theory, they sound good. Again, you could get seriously hurt doing either one.

Most of us have to live after we leave the gym or finish our workout. Exercising to "total muscle failure" will prevent you from being useful at home. And, it is dangerous. You may ignore the pain signals from your body because you're trying to reach muscle failure. I know some people will disagree with me. But, take my word for it. It's not something you need to learn from personal experience.

Becoming more active is a great idea. Pushing yourself too hard, too fast can lead to burnout, as well. When you are in pain, you want it to go away. Over time, if you associate your pain with your new activity, you will stop the activity. Before you know it, you will be back in the old lifestyle you were trying to get away from. If that does happen, just start again. What you do is up to you. Give yourself time. You'll see the changes. Don't get discouraged because, "It's not happening fast enough." Stick with it. You WILL benefit from becoming more active.

WHY

Tess had been married for eight years. She had two sons, five and six years old. Her marriage was typical with its' ups and downs. Tess had worked in a law office for 10 years and things were good there. Her husband had been working in construction for 12 years. He enjoyed his job, as well. Their sons were happy kids.

Her husband hung out at the neighborhood bar about once a week to watch a game or just hang out with his buddies. Tess was fine with that because she would usually do a "girls night" on the same night. All of a sudden, her husband's bar night began to change within the same week. He always had a different reason for the change. One time, he changed the day and Tess forgot to tell her girlfriends. At the last minute, she called Jessica to let her know about the change. Jessica's husband answered the phone. Tess apologized for the late notice and told him about the change. He was surprised. He told her the guys were still meeting on Wednesday. Tess said that she must have misunderstood her husband and hung up the phone. She went to the bar, Tuesday, the new boy's night, to see what was going on.

Stop Beating That Lady

Tess found her husband laughing and talking, in a booth, with a woman. Tess was pissed and shocked. She walked up and introduced herself to the lady. The lady could not hide her surprise, when Tess said she was his wife. Of course, her husband was speechless. At home, he denied anything was going on between him and the lady. He said they were just friends. Tess knew her husband and she could tell when he was lying. And he was lying. The more he tried to convince her, the bigger the hole became that he had dug for himself.

Three years later, they were divorced. Tess had a good circle of friends. They had been very supportive when she went through her divorce. Now, they were trying to help her move forward.

Tess was still pleased with her job and her sons were fine. But Tess only went to work and came home. A real personal life was missing. She decided it was time for a change. She didn't know what she wanted to do but she wanted to do something. Any time one of her friends asked her to do something, she did. It was fun and exciting trying new things. She tried several cardio exercise plans. She played golf, tennis and softball but she still felt she hadn't found the thing that was right for her. Then one day, she was helping one of her son's with a school project. Her son needed a few photos for his project. As she helped him get the right photos, she discovered she like the creative process of taking a good photo.

She bought a digital SLR camera and started taking pictures. A year later, she had become an extremely good amateur photographer. She had fallen in love with photography. She even sold some of her photos to a local magazine. Tess won third place in a national photo contest, too.

Until she helped her son with his project, she had never even thought about photography. Taking pictures was the lifestyle change Tess was looking for. Photography allowed Tess to tap into her creative side. It was a side she had forgotten existed.

RUN AWAY

Ruth was single, doing well, and had good friends. She was a little overweight but felt good about herself. Ruth and her friends would get together and hang out on a regular basis. They always had a good time with plenty of laughs.

One day, Ruth received a distressing phone call at work. Her friend, Jennifer, just had a stroke! Ruth was shocked. A stroke? They were the same age and way too young for a stroke. Ruth believed, strokes happened to old unhealthy people. On her way to the hospital, she didn't know what to expect. She started to cry. With her eyes closed and crying, Ruth could see Jennifer's smiling face, the last time they were together. Then Ruth had a distressing thought. She could have a stroke, too. Ruth and Jennifer's lives were duplicates of each other. Ruth wondered if she could prevent her own stroke. Right there in the cab, Ruth decided things had to change. She was not going to have a heart attack or stroke, like Jennifer.

A week after Jennifer's stroke, Ruth began her lifestyle change. She began by eating better. But she had no idea what activities she might like. Ruth told herself, she was too heavy to run. So that was not an option. She tried swimming but the water hated her hair. One of her girlfriends liked to walk, so Ruth joined her but that wasn't it either.

A few months had gone by since Jennifer's stroke. Ruth visited with Jennifer on a regular basis. It was hard for Ruth to see her independent friend struggle. But Jennifer was making good progress. Ruth and Jennifer laughed at Ruth's experiences trying to become more active. Although Ruth hadn't found her "stand out" activity, she had become more active and lost a few pounds. The biggest surprise for Ruth was that she was having fun. She enjoyed being more active. She even liked her job more.

While Ruth and her friends were having dinner, someone mentioned a charity event for the hospital where Jennifer had been treated for her stroke. They thought it would be a nice way to show support for Jennifer by participating. The event was a 5 & 10 K run or walk and a half marathon. Jennifer was really touched by her friends' plan. She knew none of them were very athletic and that meant a lot to her.

At the event, Jennifer's friends ran into other participants that they knew. Knowing a few more participants made it more fun. Everyone was pretty hyped up. They fed off of each other's energy. The friends they met there were going to run the 5K. Caught up in the excitement, Ruth decided she would try running the 5K instead of walking. About halfway through the 5K, Ruth was done. She could not run any further. She wasn't disappointed. She surprised herself, and walked the remaining distance. Ruth was proud that she had run, at all. When she told Jennifer what happened, Jennifer couldn't believe Ruth had run anywhere, especially a 5K. They both had a good laugh. A year ago, they would've said running was something other people did, not them. Ruth told Jennifer, she really liked the feeling she got when she ran. She couldn't understand it, but it was a "freeing" feeling. Ruth started running everyday. She ran just a little at first but she ran. Ruth made a few new friends that liked to run, too. The additional encouragement from her new friends made it more exciting.

It has been three years since Jennifer's stroke. Jennifer has, basically, recovered. Only Jennifer and her close friends know her of permanent changes. As soon as she was able, Jennifer started running with Ruth. It was hard at first. But Ruth stuck with Jennifer, so she wouldn't give up. Now they both run marathons and half marathons. They have never felt better. And at every race their friends are, on the sidelines, cheering them on. Running, even though none of them would've predicted it, has become a rallying point for them.

By the way, the rest of the group still doesn't run. They now participate in their own activities. But they are all much healthier and happier than they were three years ago.

HER CHOICE

Gina and her husband had been married for 12 happy years. Gina worked full time in sales and her husband worked full time at a local tech company. Gina traveled regularly, as part of her job. She always looked forward to coming back home to see her husband. But she really enjoyed traveling and seeing new things. When she returned home, Gina and her husband would swap stories about their week. They always enjoyed their weekends together. That had been their routine for about five years.

Gina had a two-hour layover in Minneapolis. During her layover, she overheard a conversation that made her rethink her life and marriage. The two people having the conversation traveled for their jobs, too. They questioned the quality of their personal lives because they were away from home most of the time. They thought that if they had spent more time at home, their lives would've been more satisfying. Gina asked herself, could they be right?

Gina and her husband were happy. But, she thought, maybe she should be home more. Gina had a lot of flexibility in her job. She didn't have to travel as much as she did. She just liked it. She liked doing things with her husband, as well. Gina decided to rearrange things at work so she could change her personal lifestyle. Her husband told her if that was what she wanted, he was all for it.

In the early years of their marriage, Gina and her husband enjoyed going dancing. At some point, they stopped dancing. Neither of them could remember why they stopped. They never had dance training or anything formal. They just liked going out and dancing to the music. Gina signed them up for a dance class that met once a week. They loved the dance class. After a couple of weeks in class, they began going out to dance a couple of nights a week. Gina was having fun but her body ached in places she never thought about. By the end of a night of dancing, she would be exhausted. When she got tired, her dancing would get sloppy and she didn't like it. She had to correct that right away.

Gina decided she needed more exercise, as part of her lifestyle change. Gina was always the type of person who wanted to be able to physically do whatever she decided to do. She started working out in a traditional gym. It was ok but just ok. She tried some of the more extreme exercise programs, as well. They were effective but she was so sore, she couldn't dance well. So they were out. Then she tried a couple of the dance cardio workout classes. They were just what she was looking for and she got to dance! Gina dragged her husband to her exercise classes. He just went along so she would feel good. He figured he'd go to a couple of classes and she would let him off the hook. After his second class, he wanted to attend just as much as Gina. He couldn't believe it. He enjoyed the classes! Seeing the joy in his wife's face was an unexpected bonus.

Gina and her husband were having a great time dancing and exercising together. Gina's choices were really paying off, at work and at home. Gina's friends commented on how much more relaxed she seemed. Gina thought that was funny because she was more active than she had ever been. Her husband also liked how much better he felt. He had a lot more energy.

It has been two years since Gina decided to make her lifestyle change. Gina and her husband, from time to time, even compete in amateur dance competitions. They have always loved to dance and now they are better than they ever dreamed. Her husband told her he was glad that she wanted to change their lifestyle. Before their lifestyle change, he was happy just being with her, but she was right. He told Gina, he didn't think it was possible, but he loved her even more than he did before. That's all Gina needed to hear. She too, was happy about her lifestyle change. Whenever Gina has a rough day, she replays her husband's loving comment in her head, and things don't seem as bad.

WEIGHT FOR ME

A lot of women have a fear of weights. They believe if they include weights in their workout, their bodies will start to look like a male bodybuilder. I have no idea why that belief is so prevalent, but it is simply not true. Bodybuilders, male and female, work their bodies extremely hard for hours a day to get the desired results that you see. They do not get their bodybuilder's body by accident.

Adding weights to your workout can be very helpful. After you have begun exercising on a regular basis, changing things up with a little weight can be rewarding. Notice I said, a "little" weight." It does not take a lot of weight to get results. In the early stages of exercising, your body is not used to handling extra weight. Therefore, a small amount of weight will make a big difference. Plus, a small amount of weight is safer. You may not know how much weight your body can handle. So be careful. Too much weight too fast can cause serious injuries. Remember, you can always adjust the weight based on how you feel that day. Do not assume the same amount of weight that works for one body part will work for a different part of the body.

There are basically two types of weights, "Free" and "Mechanical." There are pros and cons for both types. Barbells and dumbbells are the most familiar "free" weights. They are the bars with weights on each end. A barbell is the long bar and the short bar is a dumbbell. A "free" weight is one that is not connected to anything. The "Mechanical" weights are better known as weight machines. The weights are permanently connected to some type of mechanical device. Both are good and will produce results. Try them both.

When you use "free" weights more of your body is involved in the movement. For example, if you have a weight in one hand and you're bending your elbow to bring the weight up to your chest, you are working more than your arm muscles. Your feet and leg muscles are working to keep you body steady. Your stomach and lower back muscles are working to counter the extra weight on one side of your body. In addition, your upper back muscles are stabilizing your upper torso in conjunction with your core muscles. So you see, there is a lot going on at the same time.

You do not need to run out and buy a bunch of weights to get started. To get started, try using items already in your home. A plastic milk jug is a great start. Bend your arm with a gallon of milk a few times. It works. It's easy to adjust the weight, too. Just pour out some of the liquid until you find the weight that works for you. Pet lovers try using a bag of pet food or kitty litter. Or use canned goods. Try walking around with a full plastic jug in a backpack. Then wear the backpack the next time you go grocery shopping. It's easy and you can take it off at any time. You get the idea. Anything with a little weight can be used as "free" weights. Have fun with it.

When you use "mechanical" weights (weight machines), you should still apply the same rule. Start with a small amount of weight. Weight machines keep the weight stable but misuse or too much weight can still cause an injury. The stability allows the machines to be designed to work a specific muscle or muscle group.

Adding weight to your exercise regime will burn fat faster. When you use weights, your muscles break down and rebuild stronger to accommodate the new weight. Your body fat is burned faster because the rebuilding process continues after you stop working out. In other words, your metabolism increases when you exercise. So ladies, do not be afraid to use weights. Mixing in weights can enhance your lifestyle change. Some days use weights with your exercises. Other days do the same exercises without weights. Keep your body guessing. Your workouts do not have to be all one thing or the other. It's your choice if you use weights but there is nothing to fear.

DO WHAT - WHERE

Increasing your activity does not always have to be a big deal. There are small activities you can add to your daily routine that will enhance your overall activity level. We've all heard the suggestion to park further away from the store, to increase how far we walk. That is a good idea. Here are a few more:

The next time you get gas, do calf raises while the pump is running. Just stand there and raise your heels, up and down. Do them until the pump stops. It doesn't matter how many you do. You can also perform calf raises while you're sitting down at your desk or at a table. Break up your day by doing calf raises for three minutes, at a time.

Put on a song you like and dance to it. It doesn't matter if you can dance or not. Just move to the music, the full length of the song. When it's a song you like, you will not focus on the activity. You'll just enjoy it. If you have children, have them join you. Most kids will enjoy dancing around. Take a lesson from them. Just have fun.

Stop Beating That Lady

When you talk on the phone, stand up and walk around, if possible. Standing takes more energy than sitting or lying down.

While you're waiting in a drive-thru line, put your palms together, lift your elbows and press your hands together as hard as you can. Hold it for 10 seconds and slowly release. Try that a few times. Your arms will thank you.

On a random day, while you're running errands, do five to ten squats every time you get out of the car. It may look a little strange but the oddity of it will make you smile. And smiling is good for you.

Don't try to schedule these types of activities. Just do them, when you think of it. The more you do them, the more often they will come to mind. Mixing in activities, like these, will boost your metabolism, lower your stress level and improve your fitness. Aren't those some of the reasons you wanted a more active lifestyle?

WATCHED

When I lived overseas, I could not speak or read the language. But, it was exciting to be in a foreign country. It was a great opportunity to learn about another culture. I wanted to explore the whole country. I wanted to know what the locals thought life was like in America. I didn't want their political views. I wondered what they believed the average American's life was like.

I wasn't naïve. Just because I was excited and wide-eyed, didn't mean I couldn't get knocked in the head and robbed or worse, if I wandered into the wrong part of town. The city I was in was just like any big city in America with subways, buses and taxis. Since I couldn't read or speak the language, it would be easy to get lost or be misdirected. But I wanted to explore. If I rode public transportation, after a few miles, I would not have known where I was because the scenery would've change too fast to fro me to keep up. What to do? I was sure of one thing. I was not going to let my fear of the unknown stop me from exploring this country. New and exciting discoveries were waiting for me. I didn't know what was out there. But, it could be great, if I remained positive.

Problem solved, I decided to walk whenever I would go exploring. By walking, if I didn't like the area, I could just turn around and go back the way I came. By walking, I would be in complete control. The scenery would not change faster than I could remember. By deciding to walk, I could not be misdirected. I could change direction at anytime. By walking, I would have interactions with the local folks and learn about their culture. By walking, I could stop anywhere, any time on my journey. By not allowing others to decide my route, I would learn a lot more about the area. If I asked someone a question, during one of my walks, I could decide if I wanted to use the information. I did not have to just go along with it, as I would if I was riding in a taxi.

Sometimes I would walk for hours. It was great. One time, I noticed a "suspicious" man watching me. He kept showing up at the various places I visited. (A feeling in my gut told me he was "suspicious"). It was up to me to decide what action to take or wait until something happened. If I waited for something to happen or chose to ignore my gut, I would have given control to the "suspicious" man. He had his own plan and was following it. I decided to keep control. I changed direction and walked directly toward him. As I walked, I looked him straight in his eyes. I wanted to make sure he knew I was aware of him and not just looking around. After I had walked passed him, by six or seven feet, I stopped and turned around to look him in the face, again. Low and behold, he had turned toward me and was about to take a step to follow me. He stopped when he saw I was looking. I just stood there and so did he. It seemed like 30 seconds or more. But, it was probably more like 10 seconds. I gave him that "WHAT?" look. I can't describe the look. But if you're from a big city, you know the look. It says, "Bring it on, bitch" without saying a word. Then, I turned and walked away. I looked back and he hadn't moved. He was an older guy. Maybe my response surprised him. I like to think it did. I turned the first corner I came to and took off running. I knew I could put some distance between us quickly. I thought my chances would be better out in the open, where I could see. I figured the old guy probably had some kind of weapon as part of his plan. I had no intention of finding out what he had planned. When I stopped, I looked back hard to see if he was back there somewhere. But, I didn't see him. That day, I made another choice. I got on a city bus to go back, instead of walking. Not being able to read the language didn't seem to be a big deal, anymore.

Once I was safe, I thought, WHAT A GREAT ADVENTURE! It was exciting. It was truly dangerous and risky. Of course, that's only because nothing happened to me. My imagination was in overdrive, all night, thinking about what could've happened. By deciding it was time to make a change in my original plan, and implementing the change, everything turned out fine. If I thought about changing my plan but did not implement it, the end to that story would have been very different. And not for the better, I'm sure of it.

Stop Beating That Lady

You cannot control things that come up in life. But, you can control how you handle them. That is why it is so important, as part of your lifestyle change, you choose to control your life and what you do with it. Don't just wait for life to happen to you.

YOU MAKE ME SICK

The staff at the clothing store where I worked played softball every Sunday against the staff at a nearby grocery store. It was always a lot of fun, despite the fact that we lost every game. Sometimes, we would get a good lead but they always rallied back to win. They were just a better softball team.

After the games, we would gather at a local bar for food and drinks. We had become a pretty friendly bunch. One Sunday after the game, a guy from the grocery store was having a discussion with one of our guys. During the discussion, it was mentioned that I had attended the same college as the guy from the grocery store. The guy asked me if it was true. When I told him it was, he just turned and walked away without saying a word. At the time, I thought it was a little strange. But, I didn't give it much thought. We were having a good time.

At the next game, that guy was a totally different person. He tried to argue about plays that weren't close and that didn't make sense because they were winning. He didn't speak to me, at all. I spoke directly to him and he looked passed me like I wasn't there. After the game, he had one beer and left. Even his own teammates wondered what was going on with him. They said he was fine at work. No one knew what was going on. The following game, he did the same thing. That was when my teammate told me about the conversation they had a few weeks earlier. He told me, after the guy asked me about the college I attended, he went back to my teammate and said, "So" and left pissed off. We could not understand why that would bother him. Lots of people go to college. We never did figure out why it was such a big deal for him. But, it was.

People may frown on your lifestyle change for no good reason. I'll bet there are people in your life, right now, that don't like you. You may never know their rationale but you will notice how they treat you. Don't beat yourself up trying to figure out what you did to them. You may not have done anything. If it's all in their head, you can't do anything about it. We like to blame ourselves because if it's something we've done, we can fix it. Remember, it's not always you. Stop taking blame for things that are not in your control.

WHY NOT YOU

Eating better and becoming more active are great lifestyles changes. Both of these will help you with any other lifestyle changes you make. When you feel better, your attitude will improve. A positive attitude will help keep your lifestyle change on track. You can change as much or as little as you like. The point is, it is your choice. No matter what your lifestyle change is, the same principles apply. Do not be afraid to start. Keeping things simple, in the beginning, will make it much easier to get started. So start, now!

Most people in the world are optimistic. We hear and think more about the negative people because their negativity usually makes a good story. Remember, as you move forward with your lifestyle change, you will meet people with a positive outlook on life. Don't be discouraged by the naysayers. There will always be people ready to tell you why you shouldn't make a change. Once they reveal that to you, limit your contact with them.

Have you ever wondered why someone that, you believe, does not have talent is doing well and may even be famous? Everyone has done it. The names will vary with each person you ask but everyone can think of at least one person. No matter whom you choose, the bottom line is the same. Despite the naysayers, they chose to start, anyway. It wasn't easy but they did it. You can too. Just start!

As eating better and becoming more active becomes a part of your new lifestyle, you will learn things about yourself. Your likes and dislikes will become clearer to you and may even change. You will become more comfortable making decisions that are good for your personal wellbeing. You will begin to see opportunities around you that you never noticed before. As these opportunities reveal themselves to you, don't hesitate to talk to the experts in those fields. You may have started small and simple, but now you're on your way. You're more focused, now. The experts can help your lifestyle change continue to improve and grow. You don't know what you don't know. The experts can help.

NOT ALLOWED

Have you decided to start? If not, try this. Put on the one item of clothing or shoes that you really like and you know looks good on you. Now wear that all evening, at home. If anyone asks you why you're wearing it, say, "Because I want to." Congratulations! You just started your lifestyle change. You just did something that made you feel better. Sure, it may have seemed a little strange, at first, because you've always felt you had to justify every move you made. If you need a reason, you did it for yourself. But did you notice the slight smile that appeared on your face when you put it on? You just made yourself happy. Good for you.

Just keep it up. You decide why and what you do. Just because, "It's always been done that way" doesn't mean it has to be done that way. Just because you've always watched TV from the time you got home until you went to bed, doesn't mean you have to. One night a week, do something else. You never know what positive effects it may have on your life and those around you.

Stop Beating That Lady

If you did not always have Type 2 diabetes, it is very possible that you do not have to have it for the rest of your life. If you developed it from eating too much crap and not being active, you can reverse it. Don't just accept it. Don't just treat it. Start eating better and get more active. It can work. Why wait any longer? Just start, now, not tomorrow.

As you start to feel better, it will become more difficult for other people to make you feel bad about yourself. Stop pointing out, to others, what you consider your personal flaws. Why help them make you feel bad? Point out something, you think is good about them, instead. It will encourage them to do the same.

Making choices that will improve your life is always a good idea. Do not allow people who are stuck in a rut to convince you to stay in that rut with them. As we have seen, some people will try to keep you there. Don't allow it. There's nothing wrong with trying to pull them out, too.

It will always be easier to, "Just think about it." It's easier because you don't have to do anything. You've thought about it, enough. You already know it's a good idea. You've been waiting, too long. In fact, why were you waiting? "Because?" Stop it. Start, now. If someone was going to start with you but they haven't quite come around, start without them. By choosing to start now, you may get them to join you, per the original plan. But, what if they don't join you? You've got it. Keep going, anyway!

You know what resistance you may face by choosing to improve your lifestyle. The benefits are just too great to just sit there. You really CAN do it! Start today. Make choices that will change your life for the better. No matter how small you may think the step is, every step helps. Keep choosing to move in a positive direction and your lifestyle will change for the better. There is no time requirement. Take the time necessary. Just start!

Stop Beating That Lady

<u>MY PLAN</u>
Start now!

www.ingramcontent.com/pod-product-compliance
Lightning Source LLC
Chambersburg PA
CBHW031457040426
42444CB00007B/1131